**Learning Tree
1 2 3**

What Happened?

orthcott

By Natalie Swift

strated by Bernard Robinson

CHERRYTREE BOOKS

Read this book and see if you can answer the questions at the end. Ask an adult or an older friend to tell you if your answers are right or to help you if you find the questions difficult. Often there is more than one answer to a question.

A Cherrytree Book

Designed and produced by
A S Publishing

First published 1993
by Cherrytree Press Ltd
a subsidiary of
The Chivers Company Ltd
Windsor Bridge Road
Bath, Avon BA2 3AX

Copyright © Cherrytree Press Ltd 1993

British Library Cataloguing in Publication Data
Swift, Natalie
    What Happened?—(Learning Tree 123 Series)
    I. Title   II. Series
    909

    ISBN 0-7451-5208-2

Printed and bound in Italy by L.E.G.O. s.p.a., Vicenza

What happened yesterday?
Did you go to school?
What did you have for tea?
Try to remember.

Can you remember what happened last week,
last month, last year?
Find things that show what you did yesterday.
Find things that show what you did last year.

Ask older people to tell you about times you
cannot remember.
What happened when you were a baby?
What were times like before you were born?

My time line by Susan Peters

1986	1988	1989	1990	
15 March I was born	July My brother Andrew was born	September I started going to play group	March We went to the circus for my birthday	September I started going to School

Tell the story of your life.
Make a chart showing the most important
things that have happened to you.
These are the main events of your life.

1991		1992				1993
March I got a puppy for my birthday	September Andrew started playgroup	July I won the skipping race at School sports. Mum got her degree	August We went to Spain for our holidays		September Andrew started School. I went up to Mr Smith's class	March I had a birthday party. Mum Started her new job

Put dates on your chart.
Put pictures on it too.
Your friends can read your life story and look
at the pictures.

Long ago people could not read and write.
They had to tell each other what happened in
their lives and in the past.

Storytellers told children and grown-ups about
famous people and places.
They made their stories exciting.
Sometimes they made the heroes bigger and
braver than they really were.
They did not always tell the truth.

It is hard to tell if a story is true.
People who study history try to find the truth.
They look for things that will tell them for sure
what happened in the past.
They look for evidence.

Often people write down what happens for other people to read.
They write letters or diaries.
They write books and newspapers.
These are all written records.
They are evidence.

Pictures and photographs
are also records.
See if you can find pictures
of people who lived before
you were born.

What do they tell you about
the people?
Look at their clothes.
Look at what they are doing.
Look at the places they
are in.

Ask questions like these.
How long ago did the people
live?
Were they rich or poor?
Where did they live?
Were they happy or sad?

13

Buildings are another record of the past.
Stone lasts for a very long time.
Long ago in Egypt, people buried their kings
in great stone tombs called pyramids.

They carved picture stories in the stone walls.
The carvings show us how people lived
thousands of years ago.
These treasures are from the tomb of a boy king.

Once people built stone castles to protect
themselves from their enemies.
These buildings are so strong that they have
lasted hundreds of years.

Pottery and metal objects last a long time.
We can tell how the castle cooks made food.
We can see the armour the knights wore to war.
We can see the jewels people wore.

Wood does not last as long as metal or stone.
But sometimes it is preserved.
The Vikings sailed in wooden ships.
They had metal helmets and weapons.
They buried hoards of silver coins.

The silver came from the King of England.
He paid the Vikings to stay away.
Monks who lived at the time wrote the story.
The objects that have been found are evidence
that their story was true.

There is evidence of history all around you.
If you study it you will be a historian.
Start with your school.
Find out when it was built.
Find out about the children who went there
before you.
See what evidence there is.

More about what happened

Libraries
There are many, many books in the library that can tell you about the past. If you want to know about the place where you live, ask the librarian to help you. The library has old newspapers as well as books, so you can look up the news for a particular day or week. Find out what happened on the day you were born.

Archaeologists
Lots of old objects are buried under the ground. People who dig down to get them are called archaeologists. They dig the objects out very carefully. They clean them and then work out how old they are and what they are. Objects made of metal, stone and pottery are often found. Wooden or cloth objects are much rarer.

Museums
In a museum you will find many objects from the past. If you look carefully at the objects and find out about them, you will understand how the people who owned or used them lived. You will be able to build a picture of people who lived long before you.

Old rubbish
One of the most exciting places for an archaeologist is an old rubbish dump. Even though the objects were of no use to the people who threw them out, they tell us a lot about them. We could probably tell what your family ate this week if we looked in your dustbin. Archaeologists can sometimes see what people ate or threw away hundreds of years ago. Never look in a dustbin. Dustbins are dirty, dangerous and full of germs.

1

1 How old are you?

2 When were you born?

3 Draw a picture of the house you lived in when you were little.

4 What did you have for breakfast yesterday?

5 What evidence do you have?

6 What do you call people who study history?

2

7 Before there were books, how did people find out what happened in the past?

8 Write a letter to a friend telling him or her about your last holiday.

9 How do people who study history find out the truth?

10 Which people built the pyramids?

11 Who paid the Vikings with silver coins?

12 Why did people build stone castles?

13 This building took hundreds of years to build. It has stood for many more hundreds of years. Do you know why? What kind of building is it? What is it built of?

3

14 Make a history notebook. Write the answers to these questions in it. Write down any questions you think of about history. Stick your evidence in your notebook or in a folder.

15 How can you find out what kind of clothes people wore 50 years ago?

16 Why do you not see cars in very old pictures?

17 Which lasts longer, wood or metal?

18 Why were the pyramids built?

19 Who first wrote the story of the Vikings?

20 What sort of ships did the Vikings have?

21 Find out more about the Vikings. Where did they come from? Where did they sail to?

22 How many years are there in a century?

23 What is the oldest building in your district? Find out when it was built.

24 What is a fossil?

25 Find out the name of the Egyptian boy king who was buried with golden treasures?

26 How old are the oldest photographs? When was photography invented?

27 Choose a famous person from history. Find out all you can about them and write an account of their life.

28 Keep a diary of events in your life.

Index